Stuck
IN A TREE

Diane DeYoung

Kevin W W Blackley Books, LLC

Kevin W W Blackley Books, LLC
Copyrighted Material
Stuck in a Tree

Copyright © 2015 by Diane De Young

All Rights Reserved. No part of this publication may be reproduced, stored in a retrieval system or transmitted, in any form or by any means—electronic, mechanical, photocopying, recording or otherwise—without prior written permission from the publisher, except for the inclusion of brief quotations in a review.

For information about this title or to order other books and/or electronic media, contact the publisher:

Kevin W W Blackley Books, LLC
www.kwwilson.com
books@kwwilson.com

Library of Congress Control Number:
2014908992

ISBN: 978-0-9960839-1-1

Interior Design: 1106 Design

Cover and Interior Illustrations: Diane De Young

Printed in the United States of America

Dedication

This book is dedicated to my parents, whose daring action
to move my siblings and me from the city to the country,
fostered a deep appreciation for the simpler things in life.
It is also dedicated to my Grandmother, who taught me to
nurture and care for animals and plants, big or small. Her
love and devotion to all has made me who I am today.

In Jackson's backyard, there was a huge oak tree. It was so large that Jackson's father was able to hang two swings, three birdhouses, and build a tree house all on its strong lower branches. Jackson loved playing in his tree house. He liked looking over the edge to see how different everything looked from up high.

One day, Jackson wondered how his backyard would look from the top of the tree. Although his parents had told him not to climb any higher than his tree house, he couldn't resist the urge to climb to the top. So when his parents' backs were turned, he started climbing. Carefully, he searched for the best spots to place his feet and hands. Up just a few branches, and then a few more, he slowly inched his way toward the top.

"Wow!" he exclaimed, as he stopped for a moment to look down at the ground below. How different his backyard looked. As he climbed higher, the wind became stronger and stronger. His hair whipped across his forehead, and the leaves began to rustle loudly. He could see the narrower branches of the tree sway with the wind. He held on tightly.

When Jackson looked down again, he didn't like what he saw. The ground was too far away! He was terrified that he would fall. He was paralyzed with fear. "Mom . . . Dad," he tried to yell, but his voice was hardly a squeak, and the wind was so loud that he couldn't even hear his own voice.

Too scared to look down, too scared to move, he closed his eyes and cried. When he finally opened them he saw a tiger-striped cat staring at him. It looked frightened and hungry.

"You think you're in trouble?" asked the cat, "I've been stuck in this tree for five days. We'll never get down," he said with a discouraged look on his face.

A high-pitched voice interrupted. "What are you two crying about?" scolded a gray squirrel. "Climbing up and down a tree is easy . . . just get a running start . . . stretch out your arms . . . and leap."

"I'm a boy," Jackson said in a quavering voice. "I can't leap from one branch to another like you!"

"Well, then," the squirrel chuckled, "I guess you are stuck in this tree forever."

"I told you," said the cat.

Suddenly a blue jay flew in to check out the commotion.

"What's going on?" he chirped.

"I'm stuck in this tree," whimpered Jackson. "I'm too frightened to climb down."

"I can help you get down," said the crafty bird. "But it will cost you."

"I don't have any money," Jackson explained.

"What do you have?" asked the devious bird.

Jackson reached into his pocket and pulled out his treasures. The blue jay quickly jerked his head from one side to the other to inspect the goods.

"This will do!" he twittered. Then he snatched a colorful toy and flew away.

"What about helping me?" Jackson pleaded, but the bird continued to fly away.

"You should have listened to me," the cat piped in. "You can't trust anyone," he warned. The cat waved his tail in Jackson's face as if to scold him.

"You can trust me," a kind voice called from above.

Jackson looked up and saw a family of baby owls perched on a limb.

"I understand your troubles," called one of the owlets, with a tear running down its face.

"Go away!" cried one of the other owlets. "You don't belong here."

"You're cute!" said another. "You can stay with me."

All the owlets started chirping at once, until each of their squawks drowned out the other.

"Quiet," hissed the cat loudly, but the owlets didn't hear him, or, if they did, they chose not to listen.

Things were getting worse. Maybe the cat was right, Jackson thought. Maybe they would never get down. Jackson turned his face away from the noisy ruckus. He pressed his one ear against the tree to block out the noise and covered his other ear with his free hand.

Jackson heard an angry buzzing sound coming from within the tree. He peered around the edge and saw honey oozing out of a small hole. All at once, a whole army of bees flew out and lined themselves up in attack formation!

"Wait!" cried Jackson. "I don't want your honey. I just want to get down from this tree. I never should have climbed it in the first place and my arms and legs are getting tired from hanging on."

The bees agreed to give him one minute to retreat before they attacked. Jackson tried desperately to move his feet to get down, but he couldn't. The bees buzzed louder and louder with each passing second. The minute was almost up. Ten, nine, eight, seven, six, five, four, three, two . . .

Just then, Jackson felt a warm hand grab his ankle. It was his father.

"I have you—I won't let you fall. Trust me, Jackson. Put this foot on the branch below you," he calmly stated. "I have you. I have you, Jackson," his father kept repeating over and over again.

The warmth of his father's hand and the confidence in his voice gave Jackson the strength to move his foot to the branches below. Soon, he was cradled in his father's arms.

"You're safe, Jackson. We'll climb down together."

When they were close to the bottom of the tree, his father handed Jackson to his mother. She hugged him tightly and kissed him on his forehead.

"Jackson, you frightened me! Never do that again," she cried.

"I won't," he said. "I learned my lesson."

Jackson looked for his father. He was back up the tree. He came down with the tiger-striped cat and handed it to Jackson.

"Now you're both safe," he said.

Jackson hugged the cat and whispered softly in his ear, "I will take care of you from now on." This time, the cat didn't have anything to say. It just purred happily and smiled.

That night, Jackson's parents tucked him into bed safe and sound. The tiger-striped cat jumped up on the bed, and Jackson covered him with his blanket. Together, they dreamed of adventures and the fun they would be able to share.

About the Author

Diane De Young resides in the quiet town of Gasport, New York. She is a high school art teacher and enjoys sharing her passion for the arts with her students and family. Her love of nature, family, and childhood memories are the inspiration for her writing and artwork.

Lessons Learned

Diane De Young

Visit *www.dianedeyoung.com* for free downloads
of coloring pages with fun facts about the animals
and images illustrated in *Stuck in a Tree.*

Download the children's play script, Stuck in
a Tree, and get ideas for cute costumes.

Save 20% when you order books from this website.

Check out other books published by
Diane De Young and
receive 20% off your online order.

Contact Diane De Young to inquire about
author visits and presentations at
lessonslearned@dianedeyoung.com.

www.ingramcontent.com/pod-product-compliance
Lightning Source LLC
Chambersburg PA
CBHW042020090426
42811CB00015B/1690